ODD SCIENCE
AMAZING INVENTIONS

James Olstein

Inventions are fascinating, from wheels to cars, phones to drones, rockets to robots, to things you have never even dreamed of.

Inventions happen for a number of reasons—many occur by accident, or they might be inspired by animals and plants. Inventions are getting smaller and smaller as they go nano, and greener and greener as we think about the environment. Humans are inventing things that make them stronger and faster. And now robots are starting to make their own inventions. Scary!

This book will tell you things you will not find elsewhere. It will tell you unknown facts about the inventions that you do know, and it will surprise you with strange and wonderful inventions that you do not know.

This book will tell you what smartphones and butterflies have in common, how astronauts can "sail" in space, and why the first record played in space had to be made of gold.

Quirky, wacky, and cool—come inside the world of odd science.

For my loving wife, Becky.
Everyday with you, I learn something new.

CONTENTS

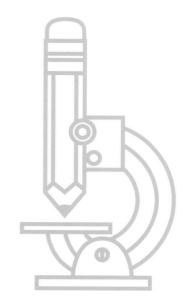

ROBOTS TO THE RESCUE

Engineers have invented a robot that is able to construct bridges using 3D printing. The bridges are sturdy and can be built in a fraction of the time that it would take a human crew. The robot can also work in remote areas where it is often difficult to carry construction equipment.

CRAZY COPIES

The latest 3D printers use all kinds of materials to build objects from scratch. Designs made out of plastic or metal are common, but some people have worked with pieces of space rock and even edible materials, such as peanut butter.

DRAWN TOGETHER

Pens have now been created that use plastic instead of ink. You can use them to draw on and off paper, making drawings in the air to create 3D constructions.

LUCKY ACCIDENT

Penicillin was the first true antibiotic medicine, discovered in 1928. It grew when the Scottish scientist Alexander Fleming left his dirty bacteria samples out while he was on vacation.

MELTING MOMENT

Percy Spencer was a U.S. army technician who studied radars in the 1940s. One day, standing in front of an active radar set, a candy bar melted in his pocket, giving him the inspiration he needed to invent the microwave oven.

NO BONES ABOUT IT

In 1895, the German professor Wilhelm Conrad Roentgen accidentally discovered the X-ray while testing out a cathode ray tube—a glass tube like a lightbulb that controls electrical current.

UN-BURR-ABLE

After noticing how tiny plant seeds got hooked in his dog's fur when they went out walking, Swiss engineer George de Mestral invented Velcro in 1941.

WATER GOOD IDEA

In the 1980s, the NASA scientist Lonnie Johnson was conducting experiments on refrigeration equipment when he managed to create the Super Soaker water pistol. He hooked a nozzle up to a bathroom sink that was able to send a powerful jet of water shooting across the room.

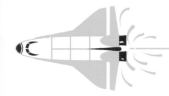

STRIKE A LIGHT!

In 1826, the English chemist John Walker was stirring a pot of chemicals with a wooden stick. When he tried to scrape the substance off the stick, it burst into flame—and that is how the matchstick was born.

A "CHEW" IDEA?

People have been chewing resins, leaves, and grains for thousands of years. In the nineteenth century, the scientist Thomas Adams was experimenting with making rubber from the sap of South American trees when he realized that it was good to chew. The first modern chewing gum factory opened soon after.

STUCK ON YOU

A researcher at Kodak, Harry Coover, invented superglue by accident while trying to make plastic gun sights and heat resistant aircraft canopies.

MAN-MADE SHADE

In 1856, William Perkin was trying to create a medicine to fight malaria, but instead he managed to make a curious, purple substance. Up until then, purple could be made only using natural dyes. He called his invention "mauve."

SILLY ME

When the production of rubber became too expensive during World War II, scientists tried a variety of experiments to find a replacement. One of these led to the creation of Silly Putty.

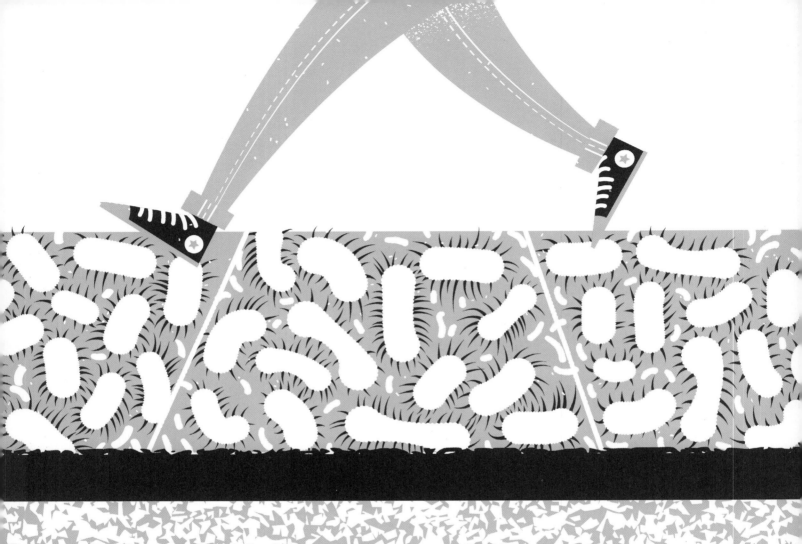

WISE-CRACKING

Dutch microbiologist Hendrik Marius Jonkers has developed a self-healing concrete. It uses bacteria to heal cracks, making buildings and roads last much longer.

AIR IT OUT

The Massachusetts Institute of Technology (MIT) has found a way to manufacture a truly breathable sports top. Flaps lined with live cells open up for ventilation when an athlete gets hot, then close as they cool down.

RUNS RIGHT THROUGH

Scientists have found a way of using live microbes to filter impure water. The microbes help to remove harmful minerals, such as zinc, selenium, and arsenic.

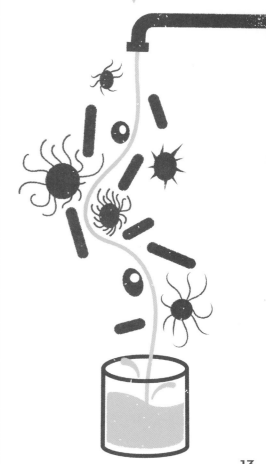

13

IT'S ELECTRIC

When Nikola Tesla studied electricity, sparks flew. His astonishing research into alternating electrical current would lead him to invent the radio, the remote control, and wireless lighting.

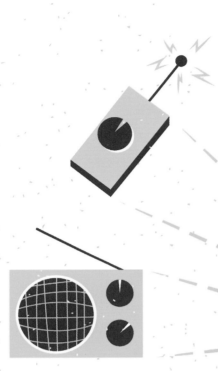

SIGNALING SUCCESS

In 1920, while plowing a field into straight lines, 14-year-old
Philo Farnsworth came up with the basis for modern TVs. He envisioned
a system that would break an image into horizontal lines on one end and
reassemble them into a picture at the other end.

STICK AROUND

Scientists have developed a super-sticky note that is ten times stickier than the feet of some geckos and lizards. Its main use is for walking on walls and ceilings. The sticky note will come unstuck when given a deliberate tug.

$2 \times 2 = 4$

$$\frac{5}{2} =$$

A BREATH OF FRESH AIR

Imagine being able to stay underwater without having to hold your breath. Scientists have invented an injectable oxygen particle that enables a person to survive without breathing.

BLOOD SUCKER

After studying the way the female mosquito extracts blood from its victims, engineers in Japan and India have created a medical needle that would make injections almost painless.

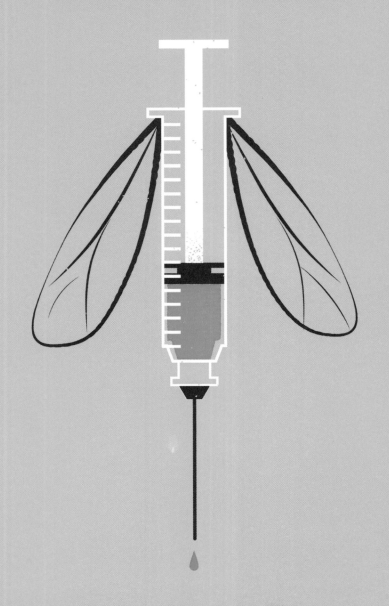

WINGING IT

The screens on our tablets and smartphones were inspired by the shimmery wings of butterflies. Nature makes the wings iridescent, so they can reflect sunlight. This reflective property makes screens easier to read both inside and outside.

REPTILE TRASH COLLECTOR

Floating space junk can be dangerous and hard to pick up. Scientists in the United States have based their latest trash-collecting robot on the humble gecko. The gecko's feet are covered in thousands of tiny hairs that let it stick onto walls. The robot has coated pads that mimic these hairs, letting it grab junk that is orbiting Earth.

SILKY SOFT

When science is inspired by nature, it is called biomimicry. Spiders have a lot of skills that humans can learn from. Modern medical tape is based on the silk that spiders make. The tape is more gentle than glue—it sticks, but it does not hurt when pulled off.

SPIDER SNEAKERS

Synthetic spider silk has even been used to make sneakers. The shoes are light, superstrong, and able to be composted when you are finished with them instead of being thrown into a landfill.

SMOOTH AS A SHARK

In 2002, Dr. Tony Brennan, a U.S. material scientist, noticed that shark skin is resistant to barnacles, algae, and slime. He used its unique texture to design sharklet—a man-made "skin" that can be used to keep ships' hulls smooth and clean.

HARD TO BEAK

The design of the Japanese Shinkansen bullet train is modeled on the beak of the kingfisher. Both are incredibly aerodynamic, making them speedy and quiet.

UP TO BAT

Bats are outstanding fliers. They flit in unpredictable directions at dizzying speeds. American scientists have built a drone that tries to match the creatures' aerial abilities. The lightweight drone works by mirroring the complex arrangement of bones in a bat's wings.

SEA SOUNDS

The U.S. Navy has studied bats for many years. Their underwater robots move using sonar signals in the same way that a bat does when it is flying at night. Sonar is the technique of using sound to navigate, communicate, or even detect other objects.

SONAR-SO-GOOD

The bat's natural sonar has influenced scientists in Israel, too. They want to use it to help tomato farmers look under the ground and check that their crops are growing properly.

HEAD BANGERS

To stop American football players from getting concussions, science has turned to the woodpecker. The bird has tiny platelike bones in its skull that protect its brain from bangs and bumps. Engineers have used this design to create a helmet that will shield a human's brain in the same way.

STICK WITH ME

One day a slimy slug might just save your life. Researchers at Harvard University, Massachusetts, have mixed up a new glue that has the same properties as slug mucus. The goo is bendy, super-sticky, and can work on wet surfaces, making it perfect for closing up wounds and other medical uses.

STRETCHY TECH

Chemists in Canada have developed a flexible medical sensor using electrodes and regular chewing gum. Even when stretched, twisted, and bent, it will still keep working. The tiny device monitors patients' heart rates and other functions.

INNER SPACE

A nanobot has been developed that is so small it could swim inside the human body to perform medical procedures.

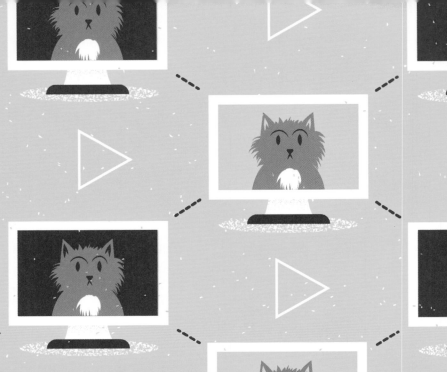

PAW-SITIVE RESULTS

Computer scientists built a network of 16,000 computer processors and let it browse the Internet to learn about humans. After a few days, it began to recognize and seek out cat videos.

CONNECT THE DOTS

In 1989, when Tim Berners-Lee created the Internet, for a while the whole Internet was located solely on his computer.

SOMETHING CLICKED . . .

The computer mouse was developed by Douglas Engelbart in 1964. Before that users had to use a joystick.

NUMBERS UP

Ada Lovelace was a gifted mathematician in the nineteenth century. She wrote the first computer program, before the first modern computer had been created. The software used complex algorithms that Ada wrote down on paper.

CODED MESSAGE

In 1952, an American woman named Grace Hopper invented the "compiler," an intermediate program that lets people translate commands in one coding language into another.

CHARGE AHEAD

An engineering student has built a wearable jetpack to help soldiers run faster. One speedy test subject shaved up to 20 seconds off his mile time.

IT'S WHAT'S ON THE OUTSIDE

An American company has developed a superstrong exoskeleton to take the strain off construction workers. As well as adding stability and preventing injuries, the suit could give workers superhuman strength when lifting heavy loads.

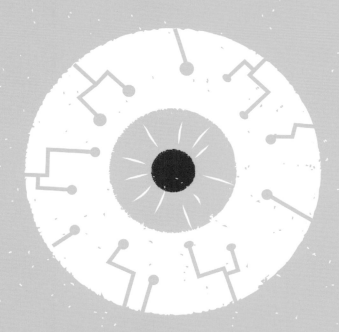

PRIVATE EYES

Surgeons can now perform bionic eye implants.
The technology is designed to work with the brain
to help blind people see again.

GROUNDED

While many look toward drones and self-driving cars for the future of their businesses, an Estonian company has created a fleet of autonomous delivery robots that drive along the sidewalk.

NO SUB-STITUTE

Not every ship needs a crew these days—the U.S. Navy's *Sea Hunter* can travel thousands of miles without a single person on board. It is able to track submarines that could be on spying operations.

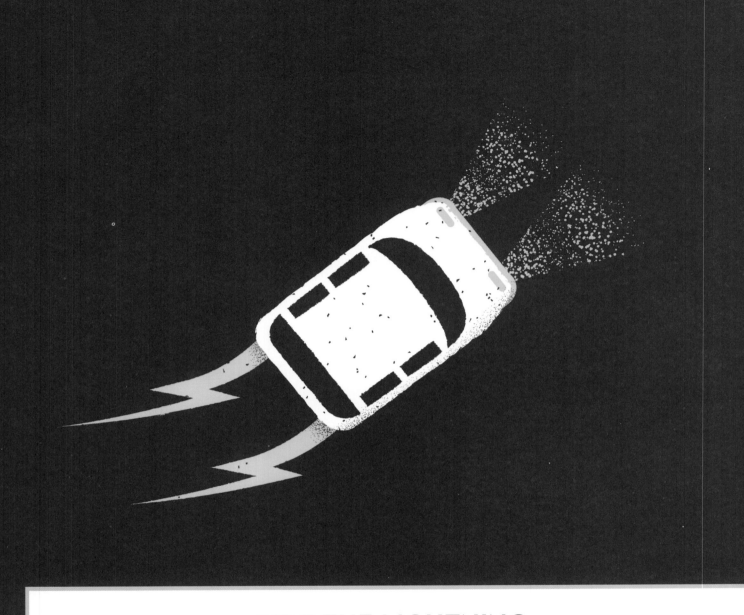

RIDE THE LIGHTNING

Pit stops could soon be a thing of the past for electric cars. Engineers at California's Stanford University are developing a way to wirelessly charge the vehicles using magnetic coils embedded into the road. The prototype has an internal coil that can pick up power while it is on the move.

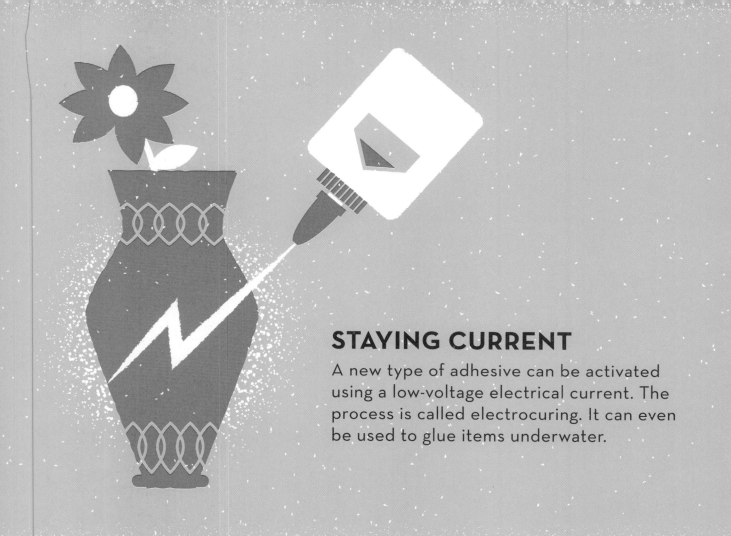

STAYING CURRENT

A new type of adhesive can be activated using a low-voltage electrical current. The process is called electrocuring. It can even be used to glue items underwater.

I THINK WE DREW A FUSE

A special ink can be loaded into markers and used to send electricity over a surface quickly and easily. When the user draws a line, electricity is conducted between two points.

SPACE TO CHILL

Advanced mirrors can now be placed on top of a building to help keep it cool. Each one works like a solar panel, reflecting heat back into space.

TREE-MENDOUS

London architects are trying to fight climate change by constructing buildings that use laminated lumber instead of materials that generate a lot of greenhouse gases. Thin layers of wood are squeezed together and then laminated with fire-resistant glue to create a superstrong weave.

SHADY BEHAVIOR

Smart glass is an innovative material that uses low-voltage electricity to make a room lighter or darker.

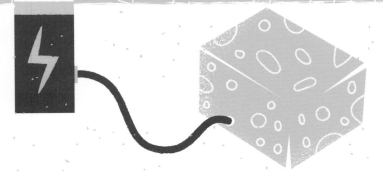

ABSORBING SOME RAYS

Solar cells convert light energy into electrical energy. The way that the humble sea sponge harvests silicon from seawater has inspired a new way of making solar cells, which could see them becoming cheaper and more efficient to produce.

WASH AND GO

Australian nanoscientists have manufactured a fabric that can be cleaned simply by holding a garment up to the light. The tiny structures in the fabric release a burst of energy that degrades marks and stains.

SUN IN

A company in the Netherlands has seen the energy potential inside our homes. They have created transparent solar panels that can be fitted instead of windows.

FOOD AND DRINK

London-based science students have invented a water bottle
that you can eat when you have finished drinking.

STREET COUTURE

Fabrics have been developed that change their color and pattern when exposed to toxins in the air. This helps the wearer to identify when their health could be damaged by pollution.

BIRD BRAIN

Many believe that the first rocket was created by an ancient Greek named Archytas way back in 350 BCE. His ingenious wooden bird was said to be capable of flying more than 650 feet. It probably worked using compressed air or steam—a method that later rockets would also rely on.

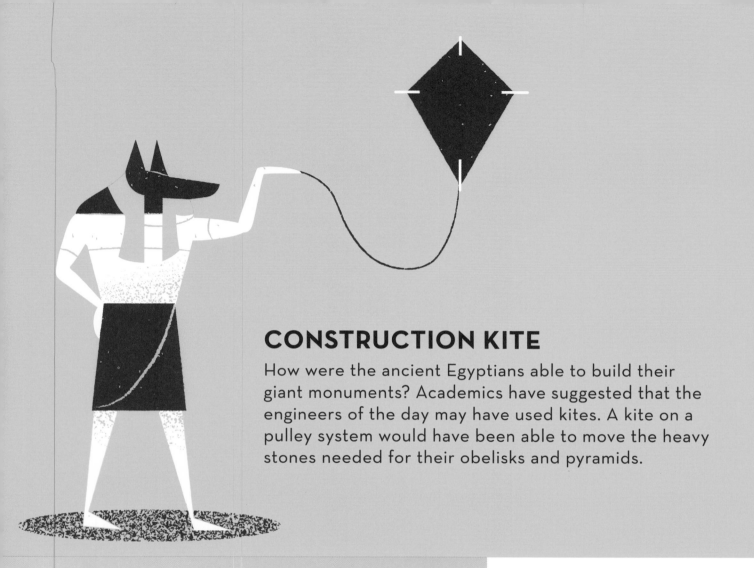

CONSTRUCTION KITE

How were the ancient Egyptians able to build their giant monuments? Academics have suggested that the engineers of the day may have used kites. A kite on a pulley system would have been able to move the heavy stones needed for their obelisks and pyramids.

WHEELY HELPFUL

Gardeners can thank ancient China for the humble wheelbarrow. The labor-saving tool was invented around 100 CE to replace two-wheeled carts that were too wide for farms and paddy fields. The barrow's single wheel made it easy to deliver supplies in tight spaces without flattening crops.

PRESSING MATTERS

Before the arrival of the printing press, every book in the world had to be written out by hand. A machine maker named Johannes Gutenberg changed that when he invented the first movable type system. By using individual plates for each letter and number, it could print multiple copies. Gutenberg's first printed book came off the press in 1455.

SIMPLY GREAT

Modern paper was invented by an official in China named Cai Lun around 105 CE. He used a variety of materials to make the sheets, including the bark of trees, remnants of hemp, rags of cloth, and fishing nets.

COOL RECEPTION

After creating many mechanical drawings for devices that dry items, such as coffee and lumber, Willis Carrier was asked to design a machine to control humidity for the printing plant he worked at. He had a go, inventing the modern air-conditioner along the way in 1902.

A HEAD OF THEIR TIME

Researchers have found proof that ancient peoples may have used their own version of painkillers. Neanderthal remedies included bark from the poplar tree, a substance that contains chemicals similar to modern aspirin.

THE EYES HAVE IT

In 1285, after discovering that light is reflected from objects instead of coming from them, "reading stones" were created by monks in Italy. They were blob-shape pieces of glass that could magnify writing on a page. They were used to read manuscripts and became the basis for our everyday eyeglasses.

SPEC-TACULAR

It is no small wonder that Charles Wheatstone is known as the father of virtual reality. He created the stereoscope, the first device that could view an image in three dimensions. The device filters the image so that a viewer's right eye and left eye see slightly different pictures. When the brain connects the pictures together, the image appears to be in 3D.

PREY MATINÉE

When researchers at Newcastle University in England wanted to see if insects could see depth in the same way that a human can, they decided to think outside the box. The team made tiny 3D glasses, then used beeswax to stick them onto praying mantises. They then successfully played 3D movies they made specifically for the insects.

BOMBLE-BEES

Not only does the honeybee have a phenomenal sense of smell, it can also be trained. Scientists are able to teach groups of bees to find bombs just like dogs.

PURR-FECTLY VISIBLE

To help find a cure for diseases in cats, scientists injected animals with a fluorescent green protein. When the team shone a light on the cats, any cells that had altered began to glow in the dark.

HARDER THAN YOU THINK

Carbon nanotubes are hollow tubes made of a form of carbon, similar to the graphite found inside pencils. The tubes are almost 10,000 times smaller than a human hair. Yarn woven from this wonder material can support loads more than 50,000 times greater than its own weight.

VEGGIE POWER

Carbon fiber is a superstrong material used in everything from wind turbines to cars. It used to be difficult to make, because much of the material burns away during the production process. However, two scientists in Scotland have found a potential replacement. Curran, a natural alternative, is made from carrots.

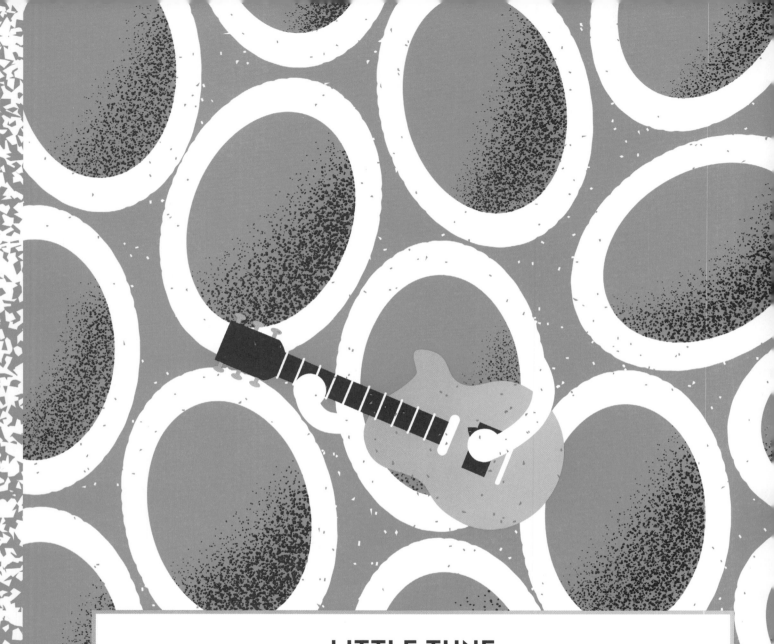

LITTLE TUNE

Nanotechnologists like to think small. American scientists at Cornell University in New York have carved a "nano guitar" out of crystalline silicon that is no bigger than a human cell. And it actually plays.

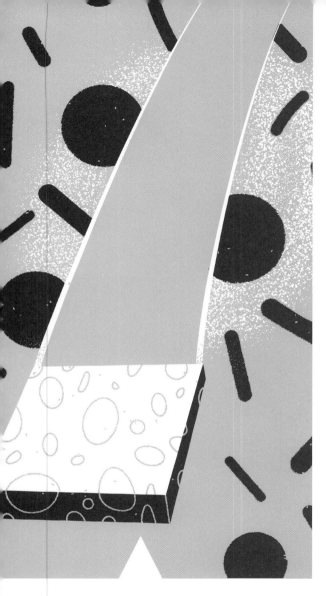

CYAN-TIFICALLY PROVEN

Wouldn't it be great if the colors in our favorite photographs never faded away? Science may soon have the answer. Danish researchers have made a special sheet of metal that stays bright when laser printed. The metal has a coating covered in tiny structures that reflect colors, so it will not fade like traditional ink.

SUPER SOAKERS

Tiny sponges are leading the fight against superbugs. The gel-filled nanosponges can be injected into the bloodstream, where they travel around, absorbing harmful toxins.

TOUCHY SUBJECT

American scientists have created a spray that can turn any surface into a touch screen using just a small amount of electricity. It can be used on any object—from a game controller to a steering wheel.

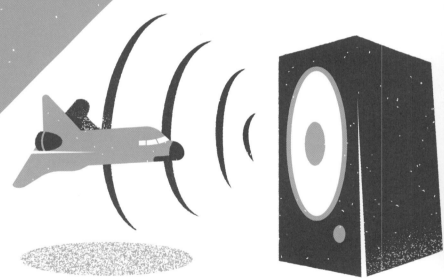

TRACTOR PULL

A tractor beam is a mysterious force that is capable of holding objects in midair. The first ever sonic tractor beam was created in 2015, using 64 miniature speakers. The speakers generated high-intensity sound waves that were able to make a bead levitate and move around.

NICE ICE

If you get hot in Japan, you can buy an ice cream that will not melt. Kanazawa ice cream keeps its shape for hours and can be enjoyed at any temperature.

59

FLOWERING FRIENDSHIPS

For thousands of years, people have been cross-combining plants to create breeds that emphasize their best traits, such as being nutritional or resisting disease.

GROW-BOT

Soft robots are now being developed, inspired by the tendrils on plants. Their movement mimics the way that real vines grow.

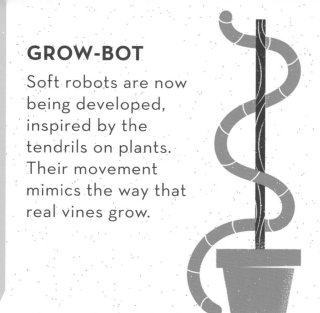

IT'S A TRAP

Nature is full of surprises. Mechanical engineering students in the United States have built a pair of robot hands that can snap shut when needed, just like a Venus flytrap plant.

FLOWER POWER

n Sweden, scientists have worked out how to insert circuitry into a living rose. The plants conduct electricity and can transmit signals. In the future, farmers may be able to use this technology to "eavesdrop" on their crops and decide when they ripen.

POWER PLANT

Plants play a key role in the battle against global warming. Scientists are now working to engineer foliage that can eat and process carbon at an accelerated rate.

PHOTO-SYNTHETICS

Some laboratories are able to grow plants that glow with their own light source.

GROWN UP

Vertical farms are helping to reinvent agriculture. In cities, these indoor sites help reduce pollution as well as producing food for the population. Instead of spreading across a large field, crops grow on different levels like a house, taking up only a small amount of space.

A-MAZE-ING TECHNOLOGY

Robots help farmers in many astonishing ways. The latest farm technology ranges from drones to crop-collecting bots, automated weeders to self-driving tractors.

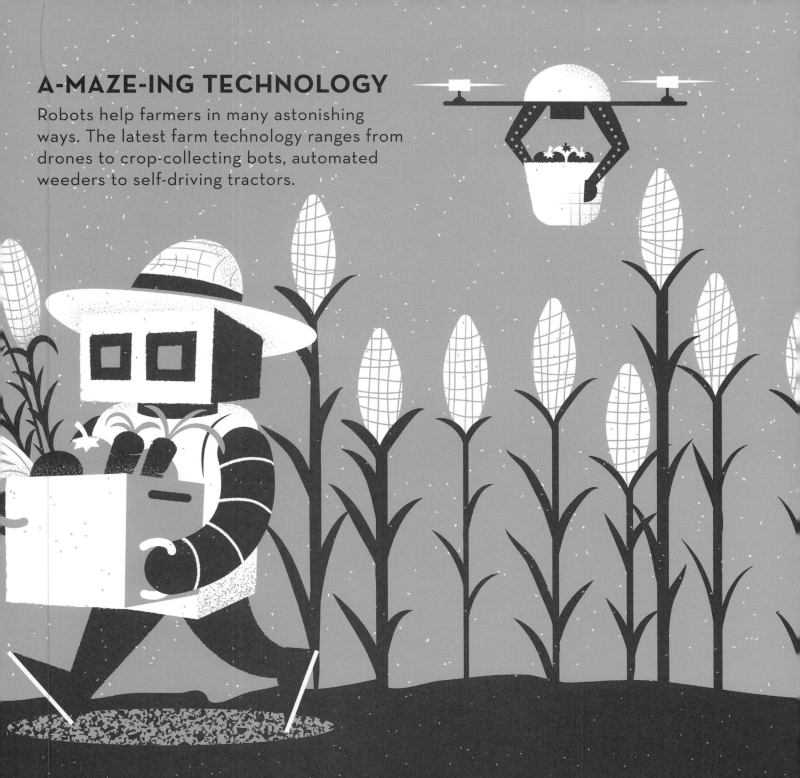

RUFF TECHNOLOGY

SpotMini is a dog-shape robot
that can open doors, climb
stairs, and deliver packages.

HANGING ROUND

Underwater robots could soon be hitching rides on the back of deep-
sea wildlife without harming it. The real-life remora fish has inspired a
machine with a suction cup that can cling to underwater surfaces with
a force that is 340 times its own weight.

TRASH BOT

The UK's Bristol Robotics Laboratory has created a robot that uses bacteria-filled fuel cells to produce electricity. Generating fuel is not a problem—the bacteria are mainly sourced from rotten apples and other waste.

METAL CELEBRITY

In 1937, the Westinghouse Electric Company built a robot named Elektro for the New York World's Fair. The 7-foot-tall mechanical marvel could walk, blow up balloons, and speak about 700 words. In 1940, he got a pet, Sparko the robot dog. Sparko could bark, sit, beg, and even wag his tail.

STARFISH SAVER

In Australia, scientists are using intelligent robots to seek out starfish that are destroying the Great Barrier Reef.

SWITCHING GEARS

Japanese roboticist Masahiko Yamaguchi has created a robot that can ride a fixed-gear bike on its own.

MADE FOR EACH OTHER

To advance artificial intelligence even further, researchers at Cambridge University, England, have developed a "mommy" robot that builds smaller robot "children." The babies keep getting smarter, because the robot learns from each build.

ASSEMBLY REQUIRED

At the Free University of Brussels, researchers have engineered robots that form groups together and vote for their own leader.

SNAPPY MOVES

Scientists in the United States have constructed a circular dome that houses 500 cameras. Volunteers are scanned as they move around within the dome. Why? To train computers how to read body language.

KARATE KIT

Teaching a robot karate is as difficult as it sounds. Researchers in New Jersey started with a bionic metal hand, a motion-capture glove, and a set of nunchucks. The robot was set to study the motion of the glove and then try the action itself. Once the robot had mastered it, this new skill could be applied to a lot of other tasks.

I'LL BE LEAFING . . .

One of the challenges in developing self-driving cars is teaching them to recognize the changes in trees through the seasons. When the trees drop their leaves, it can confuse the technology that drives the car, making it think that the route has changed.

OUT-THINK

To make computers even smarter, new chips are being developed that work more like our own minds. The technology uses sensory processes, such as the way we see, to mimic the way that a human brain gets information.

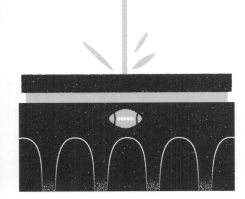

MAJOR LASER

The largest laser in the world is at the National Ignition Facility in Livermore, California. The hardware to power it requires a space larger than a football field.

SHINE BRIGHT LIKE A DIAMOND

A dazzling new laser can produce the most brilliant light on Earth. It shines a billion times brighter than the Sun.

WORLD RECORD

The first vinyl record to be played in space was John Boswell's *A Glorious Dawn*. The album and record player were lifted into orbit by a special craft using a high altitude balloon. The record had to be gold-plated to prevent it from expanding and contracting.

BON VOYAGE

The farthest man-made object from Earth is Voyager 1. This spacecraft was launched in 1977 to explore the outer planets of the solar system. It has a gold disk on board that can play sounds and images of life on Earth in case it meets alien life during its travels.

I NEED SOME SPACE

Scientists have demonstrated that an off-the-shelf supercomputer built for Earth can work just fine in space without any added technology.

BYTE SIZE

The computer on the standard U.S. space shuttle runs on a single megabyte.

ROUND TRIP

In the past, space rockets had to be discarded after a single launch. Today, some companies, such as SpaceX and Blue Origin, are producing reusable rockets that are set to make space travel more frequent and affordable.

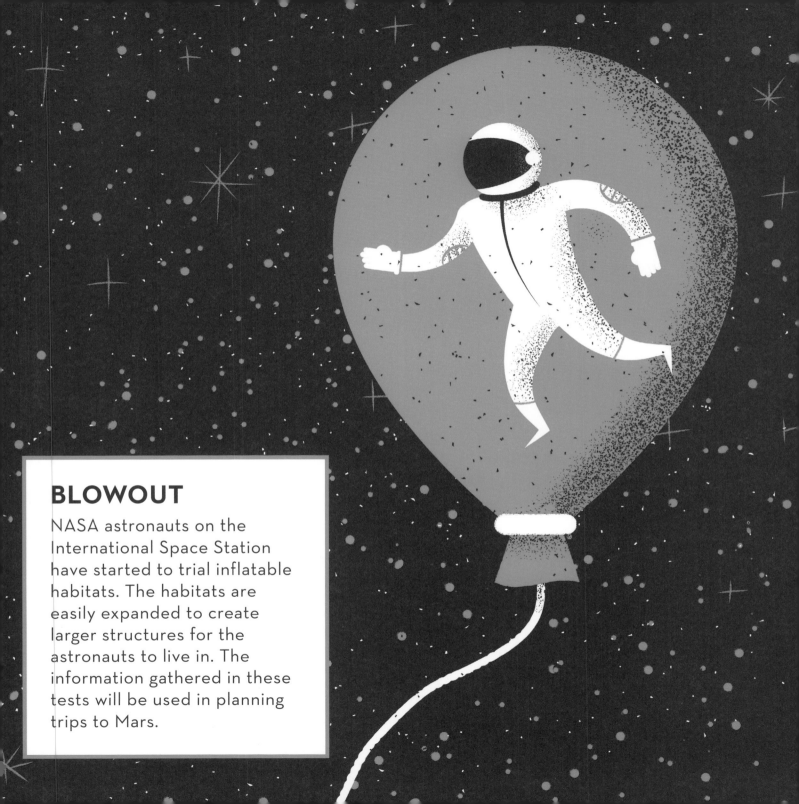

BLOWOUT

NASA astronauts on the International Space Station have started to trial inflatable habitats. The habitats are easily expanded to create larger structures for the astronauts to live in. The information gathered in these tests will be used in planning trips to Mars.

ROCKET FUEL

Scientists have created a special cup for astronauts so they can enjoy real coffee in space without the beverage spilling or floating away. The crew even have an espresso machine in the International Space Station called the ISSpresso.

PIE IN THE SKY

NASA is investigating how to use a special 3D printer to make pizza in space. As well as providing a welcome treat for astronauts, a 3D printed food system would be particularly useful on long, deep space missions.

READY FOR BAKING

German scientists are working on an oven that can bake bread in a microgravity environment. Space loaves would make fewer crumbs than normal bread to avoid starting a fire in the equipment.

SPACE CASE

The European Space Agency has launched a robot that emits lasers. It has been sent up to study Einstein's theory of gravitational waves.

THAT'S A WRAP

The Brane Craft is a thin object that can wrap itself around junk in space and then drag it back toward Earth. As it travels through our atmosphere, both the Brane and its trash get burned away by the heat.

THEY SEE ME ROVIN' . . .

On July 4, 1997, the first remote-controlled robot landed on the surface of Mars. Eight other robots have visited the red planet. There are four of them still there.

HOME SWEET HOME

COME SAIL AWAY

A solar sail offers a whole new type of space travel technology. The craft uses the radiation pressure from the Sun to make it go. When the radiation pressure hits mirrors on the sail, it creates a force that propels the craft along, like wind hitting the sail of a boat. The craft has the potential to be used numerous times to make deliveries in space.

TECH SUPPORT

Service robots are being developed to repair and refuel satellites that we cannot reach due to their vast distances from Earth.

STERLING CHILDREN'S BOOKS
New York

An Imprint of Sterling Publishing Co., Inc.
1166 Avenue of the Americas
New York, NY 10036

ISBN: 978-1-4549-3758-6
Distributed in Canada by Sterling Publishing Co., Inc.
c/o Canadian Manda Group, 664 Annette Street
Toronto, Ontario M6S 2C8, Canada
For information about custom editions, special sales, and premium and corporate purchases,
please contact Sterling Special Sales at 800-805-5489 or
specialsales@sterlingpublishing.com.
Manufactured in China
Lot #:
2 4 6 8 10 9 7 5 3 1
07/19
sterlingpublishing.com